# Cave Animals

Francine Galko

Heinemann Library
Chicago, Illinois

© 2003 Reed Educational & Professional Publishing
Published by Heinemann Library,
an imprint of Reed Educational & Professional Publishing,
Chicago, Illinois
Customer Service 888-454-2279
Visit our website at www.heinemannlibrary.com

Designed by Ginkgo Creative
Printed and bound in the United States by Lake Book Manufacturing, Inc.

07 06 05 04 03
10 9 8 7 6 5 4 3 2 1

**Library of Congress Cataloging-in-Publication Data**
Galko, Francine.
  Cave animals / Francine Galko.
    p. cm. — (Animals in their habitats)
Includes bibliographical references (p.   ).
Summary: Describes caves, the different kinds of animals that can be
found in them, and their ecological importance.
  ISBN 1-4034-0176-4 (HC), 1-4034-0433-X (Pbk.)
  1.  Cave animals—Juvenile literature. [1. Cave animals. 2. Caves. 3.
Cave ecology. 4. Ecology.] I. Title.
  QL117 .G25 2002
  591.75'84—dc21

                              2001007652

**Acknowledgments**
The author and publishers are grateful to the following for permission to reproduce copyright material:
Cover photograph by Gary Meszaros/Photo Researchers, Inc.
p. 4 Rich Reid/Animals Animals; p. 5 Bruce Roberts/Photo Researchers, Inc.; p. 6 Stephen P. Parker/Photo Researchers, Inc.; p. 7
David Lazenby/Animals Animals; p. 8 Richard T. Nowitz/Photo Researchers, Inc.; p. 9 Breck P. Kent/Animals Animals; p. 10 Fred
Whitehead/Animals Animals; p. 11 Dante Fenolio/Photo Researchers, Inc.; p. 12 TC Nature/Animals Animals; p. 13 Ken
Lucas/Visuals Unlimited; p. 14 Alvin E. Staffan/Photo Researchers, Inc.; p. 15 David T. Roberts/Nature's Images, Inc./Photo
Researchers, Inc.; p. 16 Joe McDonald/Bruce Coleman Inc.; p. 17 Gary Meszaros/Photo Researchers, Inc.; p. 18 Joe
McDonald/Animals Animals; p. 19 R. Jackman/OSF/Animals Animals; pp. 20, 22, 24, 25 Robert and Linda Mitchell; p. 21 Charles E.
Mohr/Photo Researchers, Inc.; p. 23 Fletcher and Baylis/Photo Researchers, Inc.; p. 26 Merlin D. Tuttle/Bat Conservation
International; p. 27 Jason Weintraub/VIREO; p. 28 T.C. Middleton/Oxford Scientific Films; p. 29 Gene Ahrens/Bruce Coleman Inc.
Every effort has been made to contact copyright holders of any material reproduced in this book. Any omissions
will be rectified in subsequent printings if notice is given to the publisher.

Some words are shown in bold, **like this.** You can find
out what they mean by looking in the glossary.

To learn more about the salamander on the cover, turn to page 17.

# Contents

# What Is a Cave?

A cave is a kind of **habitat**. Caves are usually big holes in rock. They sometimes begin as small cracks. The cracks become large holes. This takes millions of years, so you cannot see it happen.

Often, water under the ground **erodes** a
**tunnel.** Later, the water seeps deeper into
the ground, leaving a wet cave in its place.

# Where Are Caves?

Caves form in different places. There are sea caves by the ocean. The ocean water **erodes** a **tunnel** through the rocks near the water.

**Lava** caves are near **volcanoes**. Ice caves are in **glaciers** near the North and South Poles. There are also caves in underground rocks.

# How Big Are Caves?

Some caves are huge. Caves can have rooms larger than houses. If you put all the caves at Mammoth Cave National Park in Kentucky end-to-end, they would stretch 348 miles (560 kilometers).

Imagine driving down this cave road. It would take six hours. If you ate lunch before starting out, it would be dinnertime when you got to the other end.

# Kinds of Cave Animals

Some animals, like frogs and birds, visit caves once in a while. Other animals, like brown crayfishes, live in caves most of the time.

True cave animals are called **troglobites.**
They live in caves all the time. Troglobites
are often white and blind, like this
white crayfish.

# Cave Homes

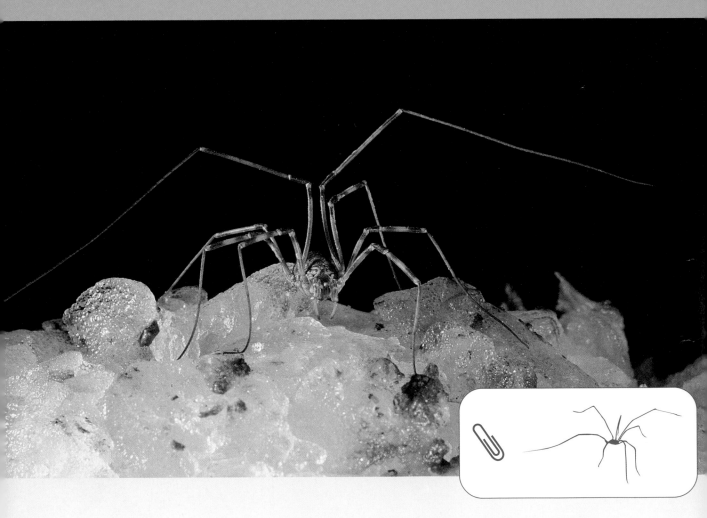

Harvestmen are spiders. But they do not spin a web or make **venom**. They live in both the dim and the very dark parts of caves.

12

Characin fishes live in streams in the darkest parts of caves. Most of these fishes have very small eyes. Some, like this one, have no eyes at all!

#  Living Near the Cave Entrance

Some birds nest just inside caves. This part of the cave gets some sunlight. Phoebes sometimes nest here. They do not live in the deeper, darker parts of the cave.

Cliff frogs have a flat head and body. It lets them fit into cracks in rocks. Cliff frogs often hide in cave entrances. They sit there and **chirp**.

Pickerel frogs sometimes live in the dim parts of caves. They like the cool water there. They leave caves to hop in the grass outside.

16

Some salamanders live in the parts of caves
that get light. They are very good climbers.
They can hold on to rocks with their tails.

# Living in the Dark

Just beyond the dim part of a cave,
it is dark. Cave crickets live here and in
other parts of a cave. Many other cave
animals eat cave crickets.

Many different kinds of bats live in caves.
Free-tailed bats spend summer days
**roosting** in caves. At night, they come
out to hunt **insects.**

# Living Where it is Always Dark

In the deepest part of some caves, it never gets warm or sunny. White pill bugs live here. They aren't really bugs. They are **crustaceans**.

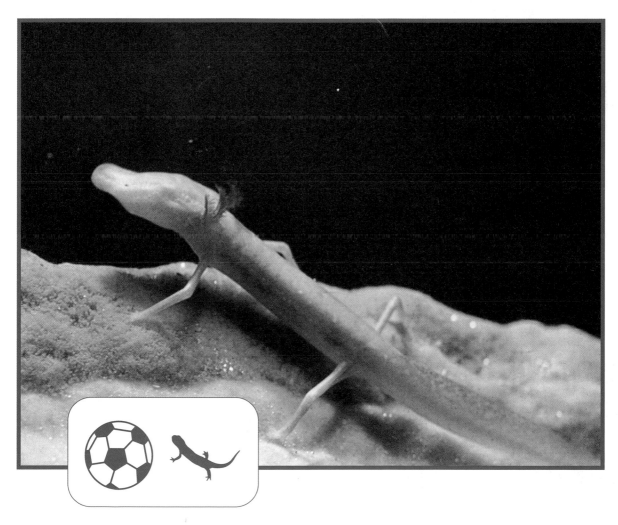

Most parts of caves are very dark all the time. The animals that live here cannot use eyes to see. The Texas blind salamander only has spots where its eyes should be.

# Finding Food in a Cave

There is little food in caves. Plants cannot grow in the dark. So what do cave animals eat? Cave beetles, like this one, eat cricket eggs.

Giant cave cockroaches often live in caves
near bats. They eat bat droppings, or poop.
Bat droppings are also called **guano**.

# Cave Predators

Some cave animals are **predators.** They hunt other animals in caves. Large scorpions sting cave crickets. Then, they eat the crickets.

Tooth Cave spiders spin webs under rocks.
Tiny **insects** get caught in the webs and
cannot get out. The Tooth Cave spiders
eat these insects.

# Cave Babies

Some mother bats form **nurseries** of baby bats in caves. Mexican free-tailed bats may have many hundreds of baby bats in one nursery.

Swiftlets live in caves in Asia and India.
They build nests from strands of their
saliva. Then they lay one or two eggs in
the nests.

# Protecting Cave Animals

In the past, people did not understand how important caves were to some animals. Some caves were **polluted** or filled in with dirt. People wrote **graffiti** on cave walls. Many cave animals were killed.

28

Today, people are working to keep caves clean and safe for the animals that live there. People even teach others about cave animals. If you visit a cave, don't write on the walls. Respect the animals.

# Glossary

**chirp** sound made by a small bird or insect

**crustacean** animals that usually have a shell and live in water, such as lobsters, crabs, and shrimp

**erode** to wear away

**glacier** big piece of ice that slowly moves down a mountain or across land

**graffiti** writing on walls

**guano** bat droppings

**habitat** place where an animal lives

**insect** small animal with six legs

**lava** very hot, liquid rock that flows from a volcano

**nursery** group of baby animals

**pollute** to make dirty

**predator** animal that hunts and eats other animals

**roost** to rest or sleep on the side of a cave or in a tree

**troglobite** animal that lives in caves all the time

**tunnel** long, thin hole in a rock or underground

**venom** poison

**volcano** hole in the ground that hot rocks and air come out of

# More Books to Read

Delafosse, Claude. *Caves: Hidden World.* New York: Scholastic Trade, 2000.

Llewellyn, Claire. *Caves.* Chicago: Heinemann Library, 2000.

Schuh, Mari C. *What Are Caves?* Mankato, Minn.: Pebble Books, 2002.

# Index